Diaries of a baby

LILIA MONTEIRO

Diaries of a baby

Diaries of a baby
Lilia Monteiro

Translated by
Phillip Barryman

Images
Lilia Monteiro

Electronic publishing
Ida Gouveia / Oficina das Letras®
www.oficinadasletras.com.br

Produced by

Printed in

For my daughter.

Prefacing Baby Luke

The birth of a baby makes us happy, trembling with great emotion. Plans for this new life are unfolding throughout the months of pregnancy.

Then the great day comes!

A beautiful, perfect baby was born, who to the surprise of the physicians and all of us, showed some limitations. Joy over the birth of baby Luke was soon mixed with many other feelings.

They were times of pain and uncertainty.

After many examinations, the diagnosis: Nemaline Myopathy – a genetic mutation that I don't think most of us know about.

When parents and relatives become aware of the disease, they understand how difficult the struggle of this warrior and his parents will be.

A power higher than all this keeps the parents firm and hopeful. Beyond all the medical care they furnish their son, they are the inventors and creators of some instruments that may help him in therapy. We follow the progress of baby Luke from a distance, and that arouses within us great emotion with each advance he attains.

Diaries of a Baby has been written by Luke's maternal grandmother and shows a little how his daily routine in a Neonatal ICU was. These are moving stories, with words and feelings that have sprung from a grandmother's great heart.

With this book Lilia intends to help in research efforts, disease awareness, as well as contribute with Luke's medical care, and it is with a great feeling of gratitude to God that I recommend that it be read.

Arlete Trentini dos Santos*

---

* Arlete Trentini dos Santos, born in the state of Santa Catarina in 1952, and married to the poet Bridon since 1969, has four children and five grandchildren. Life has taught her everything. She has received awards and honors in the literary arena. Peace Ambassador of the Divine Académie Française des Arts Lettres et Culture. Full member of National Academy of Letters of the Portal of the Brazilian Poet, Chair 14. Member of the Academy of Brazilian Luminescence/Araraquara Chair 22. Member of the Alpas Academy 21. International Academy of Arts, Letters and Sciences, Chair 14. Member of the ALAB – Academy of Arts and Letters of Búzios. Member of the SEG – Gaspar Writers Society. Associate of Literarte – International Association of Writers and Artists. Associate of Flor na Pele. Columnist of the newspaper *Sem Fronteiras* (column Literary Window of the South.). She lives in Gaspar, Santa Catarina.

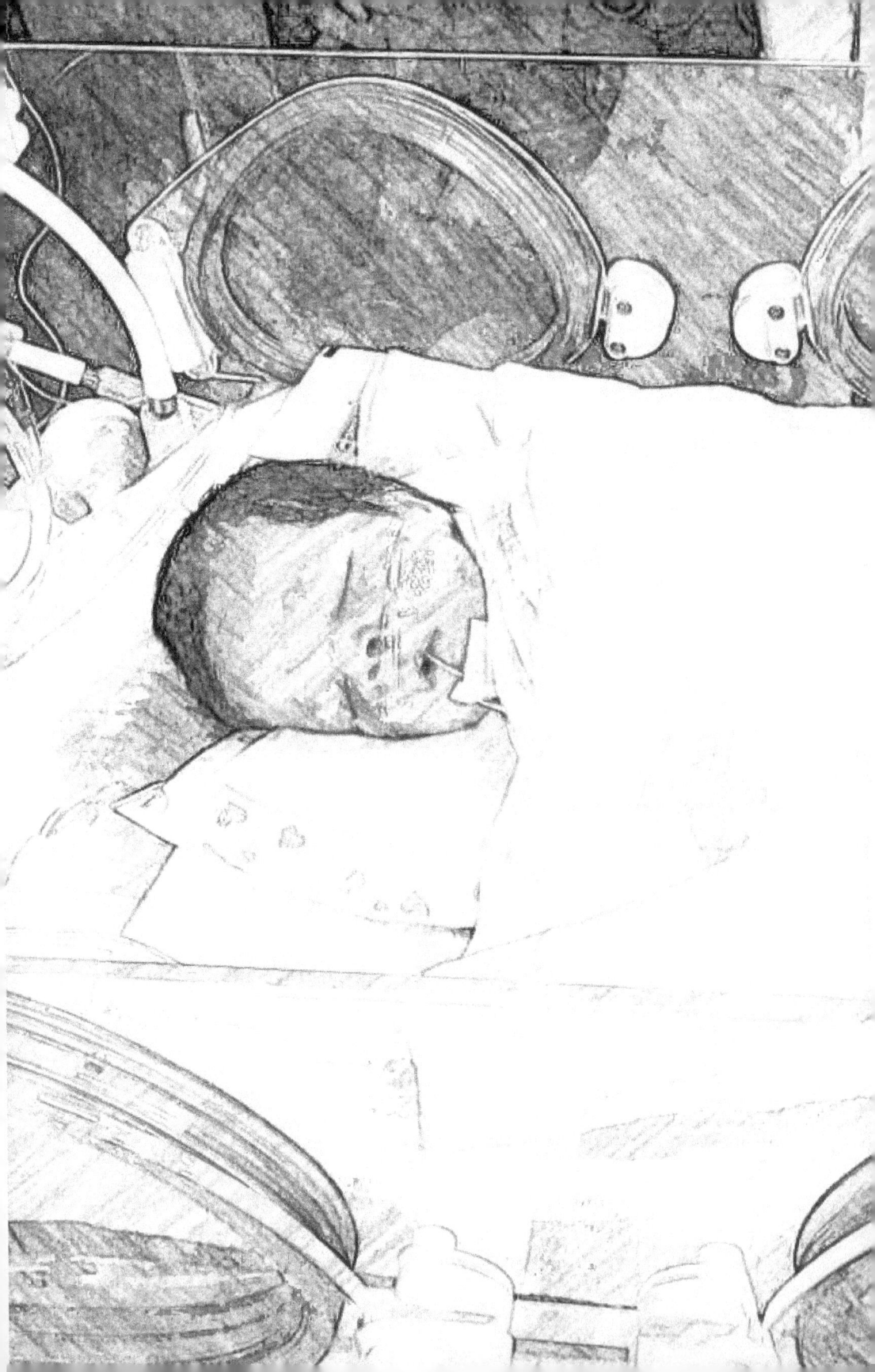

Diary of a baby

I'm here in this Neonatal ICU, together with other little friends, and many sensitive, competent and incredible people are doing various things with me. Sometimes it isn't very nice, but I know that it's for our own good.

I have a lot of hair on my head, and my mother says I look just like my father.

Mommy, daddy, and the whole family say that I'm a warrior. Someday, I'm going to understand that.

Mommy and daddy stay with me here all day. They read books, tell stories, sing, and talk with me a lot. They change my diaper, they cherish me. Sometimes mommy leaves, I think she is going to eat, after all, every two hours she has to pump milk for me. I'm fed through a tube and now I receive only milk from my mommy, which is delicious, much better than when in combination with IV fluids.

I'm getting a little better every day and I think it's because there are lots of people sending lots of positive energy, so I'll get well and go back home soon. I also want to meet our dog Bolt. My parents have already taken him a bit of clothing with my smell. I think it's for him to feel that his little brother is nearby.

That's it for today, but I want to thank everyone for all the prayers and to ask them to keep sending lots of positive energy so I and my little friends here will soon get better.

A loving little kiss for everyone!!!

Signed:

Luke

Diary of a baby 2

This hospital life isn't easy. Even though, I'm glad I'm receiving the care I need and lots of affection.

As you know, my daddy and my mommy stay by my side all day. I can smell my mother and my father also, but I confess that my mommy smells nice.

I now know my mother's and my father's voice. I enjoy listening to them a lot. My mother always says that I'm her sweetie. And I get silly. My father presented me some bands that he likes and one of them is U2. He has good taste for music!!! Ohh!!! And he also sings some songs for me. Yesterday he said that we're going to sing in the bathroom and I got very excited.

I think my father is an Ironman. I don't really know what that is, but it must be something good.

Sometimes I hear some different voices. I think they're of my uncles, aunts, grandmas, grandpas, sending me loving messages. My mother said she wants me to meet everyone, and that's very good, because I know that all these people want me to get better soon, and then when I leave here, I'm going to have to thank everyone.

Today my grandma took me on her lap. I think I like grandma's lap and I can't wait to meet my other grandma and my grandfathers too.

I now know some things. That the men in my family are very strong. And I've begun to do exercise. I think it's so I can also be strong.

Today it's been seven days since I was born and I hope that I'll soon get out of here to go home, because my dog Bolt

LILIA MONTEIRO

is waiting for me. Ohh, did I already tell you that when I was in my mother's belly, my dog Bolt was always by her side? He's a super dog!!!

I'm stopping here, asking all my friends to keep sending that vibe and lots of prayer for me and, if it isn't too much to ask, for my little friends here also.

Kisses from

Luke

Diary of a baby 3

Yesterday was a special day. My mommy and daddy organized a group meditation. I was very happy to know that so many people are pulling for me. Wow! And how many friends my parents have. When I grow up I want to be like them. With lots of friends.

Daddy has now learned how to give me a bath. I complain a little but that's okay!

My father is a good guy. And the songs he puts on for me to listen to are very cool. He sang me a song of Mamonas. And my mommy filmed everything.

Yesterday some friends of my parents came to see me. And, you know, it's always good to have visits. That makes me happy and enthusiastic. My grandma said that I already have a full schedule of visitors. Hey!! I'm liking it!!!

I'm impressed with my mommy; she never tires of producing my milk and it's so delicious. Today I put my little hands on her breast and of course my grandma took a picture. Grandma loves photos!!!!

A friend of my grandma said (her name is Ana Beatriz; her first name is the same as my mommy's) that I'm an enlightened child, and I'm quite able to bring people together and lots of love around me. That makes me happy, because we all need lots of love!

My daddy and my mommy got some encouragement today, after they talked with one of the doctors. I think I'm a little better every day. It's sweetie here, my little love there. Okay, okay!!! I just want to get out of here and I'm doing my best.

LILIA MONTEIRO

Hey! There's another group meditation today. At the same time. It's just to send another positive vibe and offer a prayer, for me and for all children and people who may be suffering for any reason or illness.

Thanks for everything and,

A big shoutout from,

Luke

Diary of a baby 4

Okay let's go.

Lately, I've slept a lot. I think it's because of the tests I've done. I'm still tiny and each test makes me tired. But I'm going to be fine.

My grandma says that sleeping makes people grow. My grandma says crazy things. But I think it's great!

She says I'm handsome and she's already taken a number of pictures of me, of my tiny hands. Have I already told you that she loves photos?

Sunday I had three visits, and yesterday, five. Everyone wants to meet mommy and daddy's sweetie.

They say that when you're born your weight drops a little. That happened to me. And every day, when they weigh me, I'm a little heavier. I've even passed my birth weight already. Isn't it wonderful? I think my mommy's milk has superpowers.

I think I've discovered why they call me a warrior. I take after my parents.

My mother has such a soft voice. When she teases me or changes my clothes, she always speaks so affectionately and sweetly. And I already know that I'm her sweetie.

I do physical therapy three times a week. My daddy and my mommy bought some very nice toys to help.

Each day we're very encouraged, because I'm becoming a little stronger.

Each day is a new day!

And finally, I'm repeating the same request as always. Keep praying and sending me and my little friends lots of positive energy. And remember, as my mommy says, always be grateful for everything.

A big strong hug!

Luke

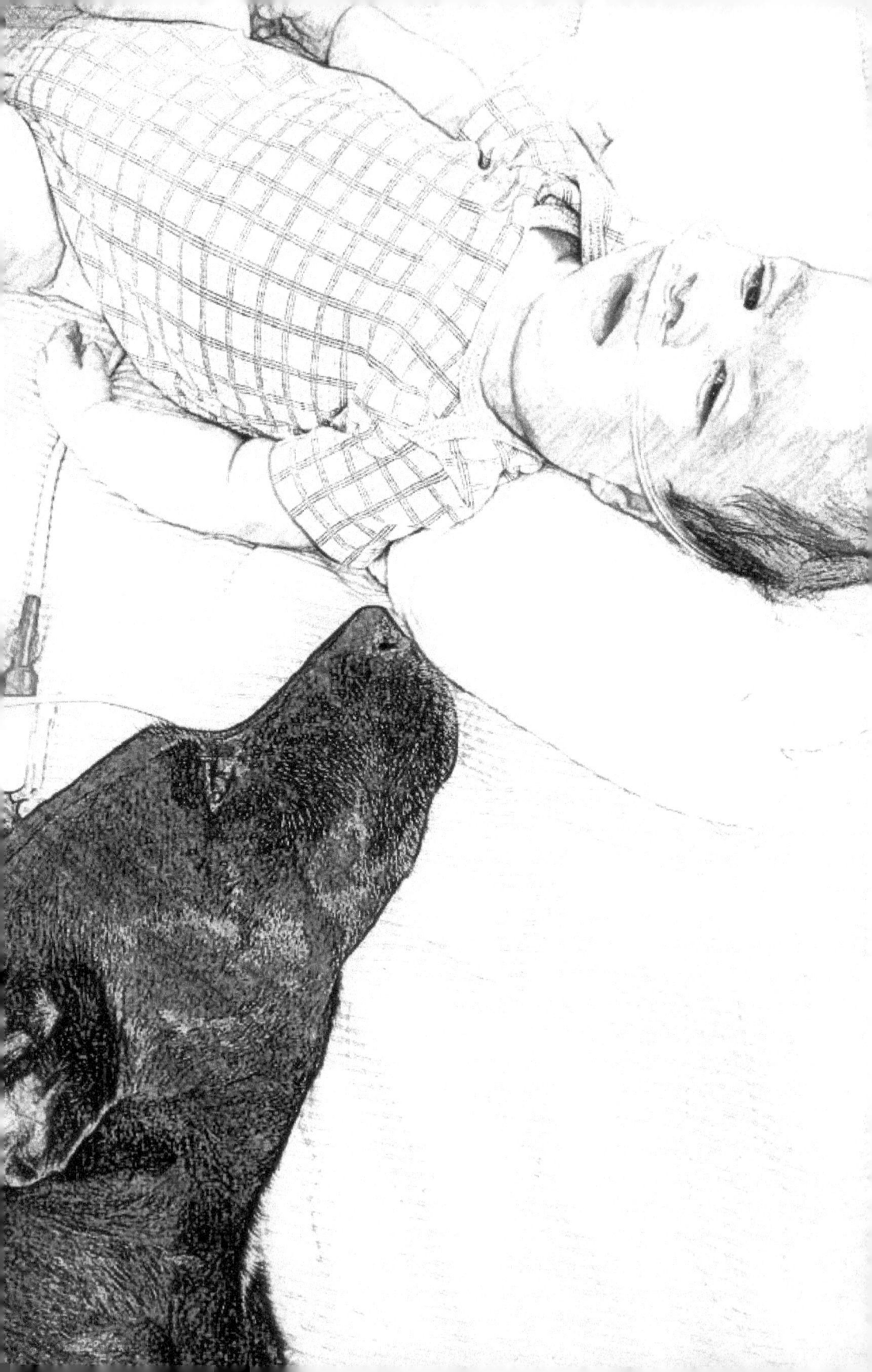

Diary of a baby 5

These days have been very busy around here. I've done various tests and on many the results have been negative. That's very good, because mommy and daddy are a little more reassured when they see good news about me. But I still have to do other tests, and as I said in the previous diary entry, each test leaves me very very tired.

Do you know what my daddy brought me? A Chewbaca mask. Chewbaca is an alien in the Star Wars series and a great friend of Han Solo. And he always protects his friend. Chewbaca makes a different sound to show love, which I like. I think my daddy wants to show me something about friendship and love.

My mother said that my Chewbaca has become famous here in the NICU, and everyone wants to meet him. This daddy of mine does everything to make my stay here happy. And I adore him.

Several things happened this week, and what I liked best was being near my mother's breast for the first time. Hearing her heartbeat, feeling her soft skin, and her indescribable smell was very exciting. And also when the nurse put me inside my father's shirt and I could hear his heart beating strong. Isn't that terrific!? I think they call this skin-to-skin therapy. But for me it's *love therapy*.

My daddy brought the photo of our dog Bolt. He is very nice. You know, I love my daddy a lot, and my mommy and I already love our dog a lot.

I think I love everyone, because love must be a very good thing.

I'm finishing up, and meanwhile, keep on meditating, sending lots of vibes and praying for me and for my little friends around here.

A kiss from *Luke.*

Diary of a baby 6

Hey folks!

This past week has been very busy here in the NICU. For a change, I did further tests, including a biopsy of the muscle and the nerve, as well as a blood transfusion.

After three very intense days with lots of sleep, I went back to physical therapy and to mommy's milk. My daddy said that I need a time away from so many tests. So I think they're now going to give me a break.

I also had to go back to the CPAP (a ventilator that helps with breathing) on higher settings, but today it was lessened. Hooray!

Everyone says that I'm a strong and combative kid, but my parents have also been strong and combative, because this NICU life isn't easy at all.

I think I'm the only baby boy in this part of the NICU. I've only seen a girl's name and pink blankets.

I have some news. My crib has been moved. I now need to pay attention to know whether I'm still the only baby boy in the room. I'm going to look into this, I'll tell all of you later.

For some time I've been trying to learn how to use a pacifier, and I think I'm going to succeed. My parents didn't want me to become accustomed to it, but it's now all part of a big plan for my recovery.

My parents help in my physical therapy and they are so careful and delicate with me. The nurses too.

Legs up and down, arms too, and I'm getting good at this. I like all these exercises because, as I understand it, they're

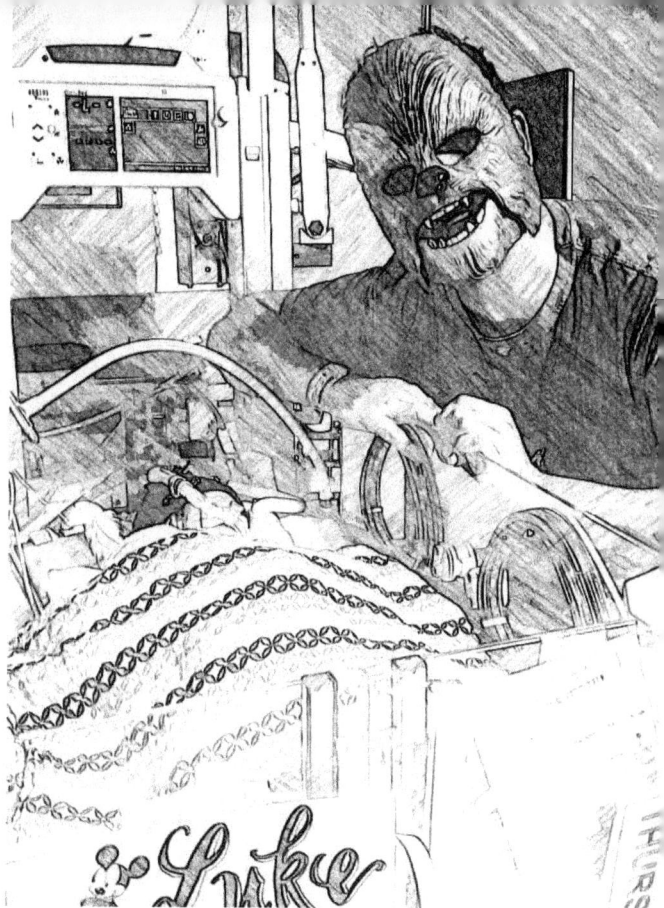

going to make me have more muscles. I think "musculature" comes from muscles, so that must be it —except very easy exercise because I'm a tiny baby!

I was thinking that someday my parents are going to want me to do some physical activity, just as they, my uncles and so many friends, who take part in some sport. My parents' friends call me "Ironbaby"! They're great, and they're all pulling for me.

You know, I've received so much love from so many different people that I'm left thinking and you're going to agree with me. The world could be one big heart, ruled by love and by kindness. Being loved is so great!

The week has been full of new things, and I know that you keep sending lots of good vibrations and prayers for me. I'm sure that all this positive energy is going to make me get better soon so I can go home.

A big "Hooray!" for everyone and thanks!

Luke

Diary of a baby 7

So many things happening and me here in my NICU crib, thinking. My mommy has always liked to write, and I know that she has also written diaries. I think I'm going along the same path.

I was born July 6, I think everyone knows, and since then I've been here at the Neonatal ICU at Joe DiMaggio Children's Hospital.

So many daddies and mommies coming and going. Wanting their children to get better and go back home.

Many babies stay here a long time, and our parents naturally try to make our surroundings as pleasant as possible, without hindering the work of the NICU teams. My parents try to make my days better, and I'm well known around here.

In my first month I earned a small celebration. My parents and the nurses dressed up as characters from the Star Wars series, and of course there was that photo. Someone took it, but it wasn't grandma.

There are so many new things in my life as a little big warrior. Do warriors have to go through all this? If that's the way it is, hey, I have to throw in my hat—I mean my little cap.

My mommy is so beautiful and kind. When she calls me "my love," kisses my tummy, I melt down completely. And she's someone full of attitude. She says I'm going to win, and that she's learning to be strong with me, but, you know, I think it's the other way around.

My daddy is very optimistic toward life and everything. And he is always supporting my mommy when she becomes sad. When I grow up I'm going to be like him, he's such a good example for me.

Here at the NICU, only two persons can come in at a time. And when they perform a procedure on some baby, everyone in here has to wear a mask and a cap.

LILIA MONTEIRO

My maternal grandfather was here these days. This week I was visited by two of my uncles, my daddy's brothers. They're strong guys like my father and they held me in their lap. It was great! I've also been visited by my paternal grandfather.

I always think that I'm blessed, because I have a family that loves me a lot and is going to take very good care of me when I leave here. But I know many children don't have a family, and that makes me sad. I still don't know how to pray, but I'd very much like all children to have a family.

The result of my biopsy came out. My nerves are okay.

My muscles, they're weak, but I'm going to make an effort so they'll get better. My parents are incredible and they're going to help me. Besides that, I've already made many friends who are pulling for me. And that means a lot.

After the biopsy result came out, I thought: I need to do something to encourage my mommy and my daddy. I'm not sure whether you know, a little baby only knows how to make demands by crying. And I needed to draw attention somehow. So the next day I cried out loud, I raised my arms and legs and twisted and turned. So much that the nurse had to hold me in her lap to calm me down. My daddy then also held me in his lap, and I was calmer. I stayed with him for a long time, skin against skin. I thought, so this is how it is, you cry and you get some lap time. It served to encourage everyone. I've now learned that if I cry enough, besides being good for strengthening my lungs, I can also get some lap time.

There's nothing better than mother's lap, and there a big surprise was waiting for me. I was finally at my mommy's breast. I couldn't suck her milk, because I'm still not able to swallow, but I can feel my mommy closer and see her thrilled over me there, up close, it was just too much!!!

Wow! That's it for today.

I just hope I haven't tired you with this long diary entry, because I've gotten very tired. But, I'm a tiny baby!

And as always, lots of prayer for us, little babies, and all those for all who suffer for any reason.

Kisses! *Luke*

Diary of a baby 8

Last week I had an operation. A big step so I can go home soon. They did a G-Tube in my little tummy, and now I'm being fed through there. This was necessary and now it will be much easier for me to do speech therapy exercises and to learn to swallow. Sincerely, that tube in my throat was terrible.

I know many people were pulling for me so the operation would be successful. I'm very grateful for all the positive energy.

I'm also grateful to all those who read my diary. As I said, I'm following the steps of my mommy who has always liked to write, and now my daddy, who is writing very nice things.

My daddy wrote in his blog that we must be grateful for everything we have. He wrote about how he is grateful for my small daily advances, which for him and for my mommy are great victories. And a simple cough of mine, for example, which they have never seen, is something sensational! I liked that word: Sen-sa-tio-nal!

Incredible that everything I do different is a reason for joy for my mommy and daddy.

I have already decided that I need to learn more things and very fast, in order to be able to feel and see my parents happy with each new thing of mine. And I'm going to succeed!

Sometimes I'm a little confused because my parents and my grandma say the same things differently. Most times my parents speak just like the nurses around here and very fast, but I make an effort and I understand everything. Anyway, I'm going to have to learn to speak like my grandma or teach her to speak like my parents.

Just now a doubt has occurred to me. Is my dog Bolt going to understand me? Ohh! That's okay.! When I go home I'm going to communicate with him somehow.

LILIA MONTEIRO

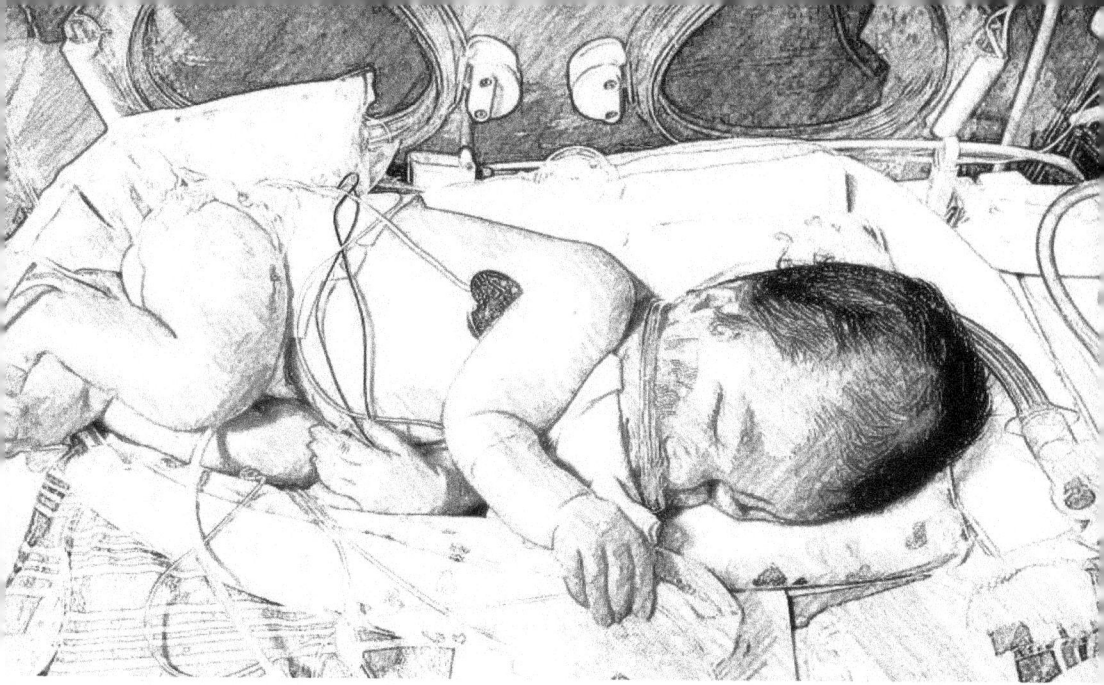

You know, dear diary, I'm still a little baby but I now think and I want so many things. I'm becoming a beggar. Sorry!

I want to ask all daddies, mommies, grandmas, grandpas, aunts, uncles and also friends to read to the children they have nearby and to those who are in the hospital, like me.

Here in the hospital, under my crib there is a mountain of books, and if anyone wants I can ask my parents to lend them. As I've already said, my parents read to me and it's very cool, besides which it stimulates creativity and makes people travel. I can't wait until I go home.

My grandma told me that she loves traveling. She also told me that she tells everyone that I'm very handsome, and that when I go to travel around in Brazil, many persons are going to want to meet me, and are going to say that I'm good-looking and strong. I think grandparents are the greatest.

Last week my other uncle, my mother's oldest brother, visited me. He's also big and strong. I liked him. My family only has strong men and I'm going to be one too. I'm going to try hard. I promise!

Lots of energy for everyone.

A kiss from

Luke

Diary of a baby

A few days ago I was transferred to another room, also in the NICU, where parents can stay 24 hours with their babies, and it works like a kind of training for going home. For the first time my mommy could sleep with me. And I slept a lot that first night. But my mommy stayed awake caring for me. She looked like a nurse.

In my crib now there's a colorful aquarium, with little fishes and music. It helps me relax and focus my attention.

Saturday September 10, there was a 5 k run and walk in Wellington, in the city where I was born and live. My daddy had hats and wristbands made for #golukewygand. My team was successful and I won an award. Isn't that exciting? Even my grandma participated in the race. Sure, she walked more than ran, but I understand, after all, grandmas are the greatest, they tell stories, they like to take pictures and record videos, and they're always saying that we're cute. So, it doesn't matter whether they run, walk, or move along very slow.

It was very cool to know that so many people took part in the run on my behalf, and in the end I won a trophy. Very nice!!!

My daddy always says that he is excited and thankful for so many people, out there wearing the wristband in my honor. According to him, it's a lot of energy and vibration for his beloved son.

I have discovered that my daddy and my mommy love each other a lot. And they also love me a lot. I think I couldn't belong to a better family. I realize that sometimes my mommy

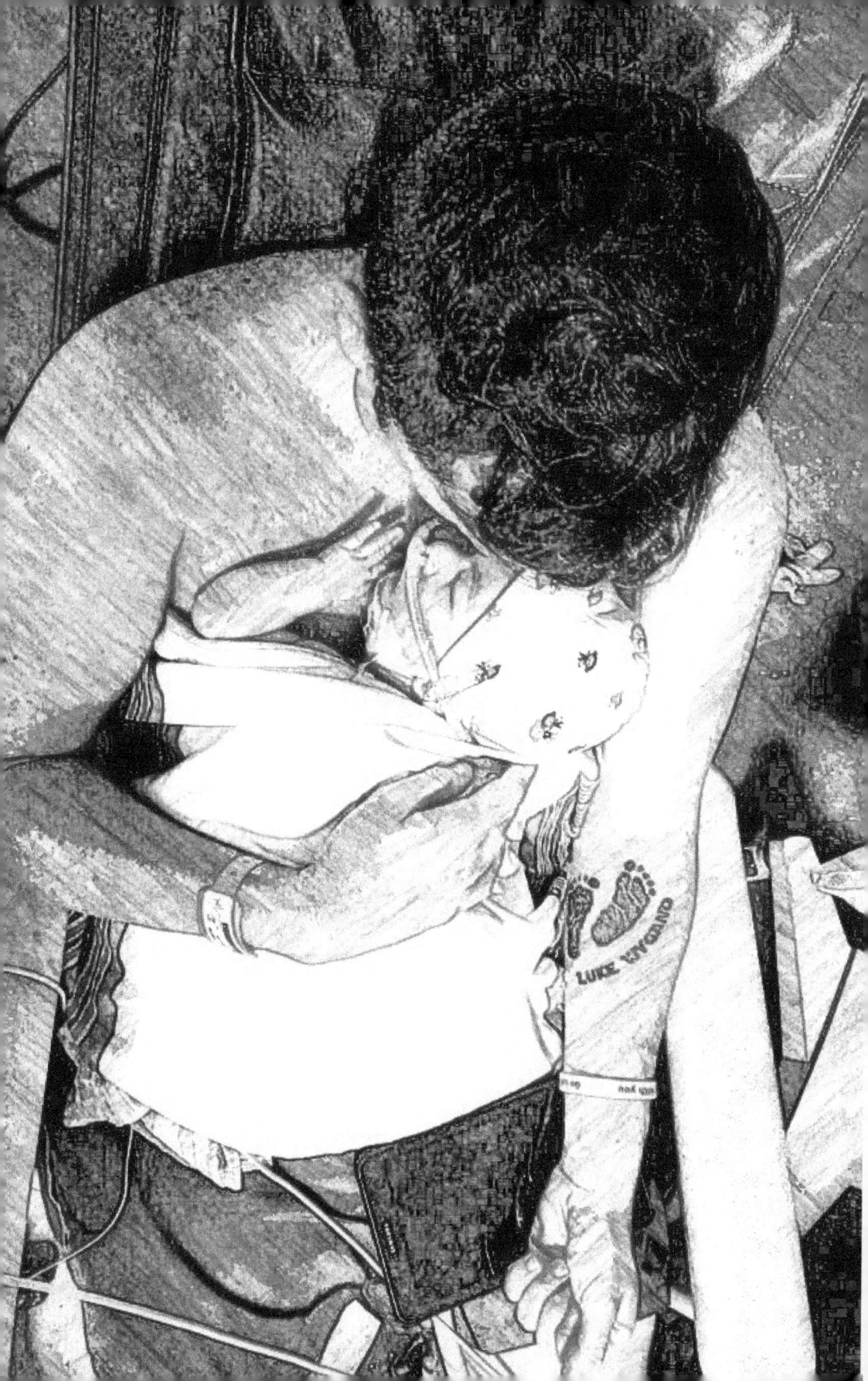

is sad, but that's when I try to do something different, and she opens that big smile.

For six days I was breathing on my own, without using that annoying thing in my nose. And you know, I've been strong!!! But I had to return to the ventilator. As my parents said, it was a marathon and at kilometer 30, I was tired, but I didn't quit, I stayed strong, like my parents, and I went to the finish line. Now I need to recover to go back to training. After all, I can't wait until I go home.

My parents are incredible. They always sing and play with me. It's always a lot of fun when our parents play with us. My parents love it and of course I do too! Their strength, their love, together with the prayers, positive energy from everyone, and of course, my mommy's milk, make me stronger every day. They always say we have to be grateful for everything we have. And I always need to remember to do that. So thanks everyone!

A big hug from

Luke

Diary of a baby 10

I'm a little baby, and I'm going to try to make everything calmer for my mommy and my daddy.

I had to go back to help with breathing and now I use a BPAP in my nose. It's a little uncomfortable but it's for my own good.

I always hear my parents say, "Our baby is here, he's going to win, and we're always together."

My parents are strong, I'm always sure of that, even though they're sometimes sad. They're strong and they will always seek what is best for me. They're going to try to make sure that more research is done and scientists soon discover how to make sure that other children will overcome this muscle problem that we have.

My mommy and my daddy have been tireless in my recovery. And I always think: we're together here!!!

My parents have done training and first aid on babies. They're learning how to use the machine that helps me to breathe better, and they're going to learn to deal with the feeding tube. All this so they can take care of me at home. I'm anxious to get to know my house, my room and of course my dog Bolt. We're going to be great friends!

Did you know that I also went through training? I had to stay in a chair, like a car seat, only more inclined, and believe me, I was able to stay as much time as necessary to travel to my house. I even did a trip around the hospital. And it was filmed and very much celebrated by everyone. My parents were beaming! Yesss!!!

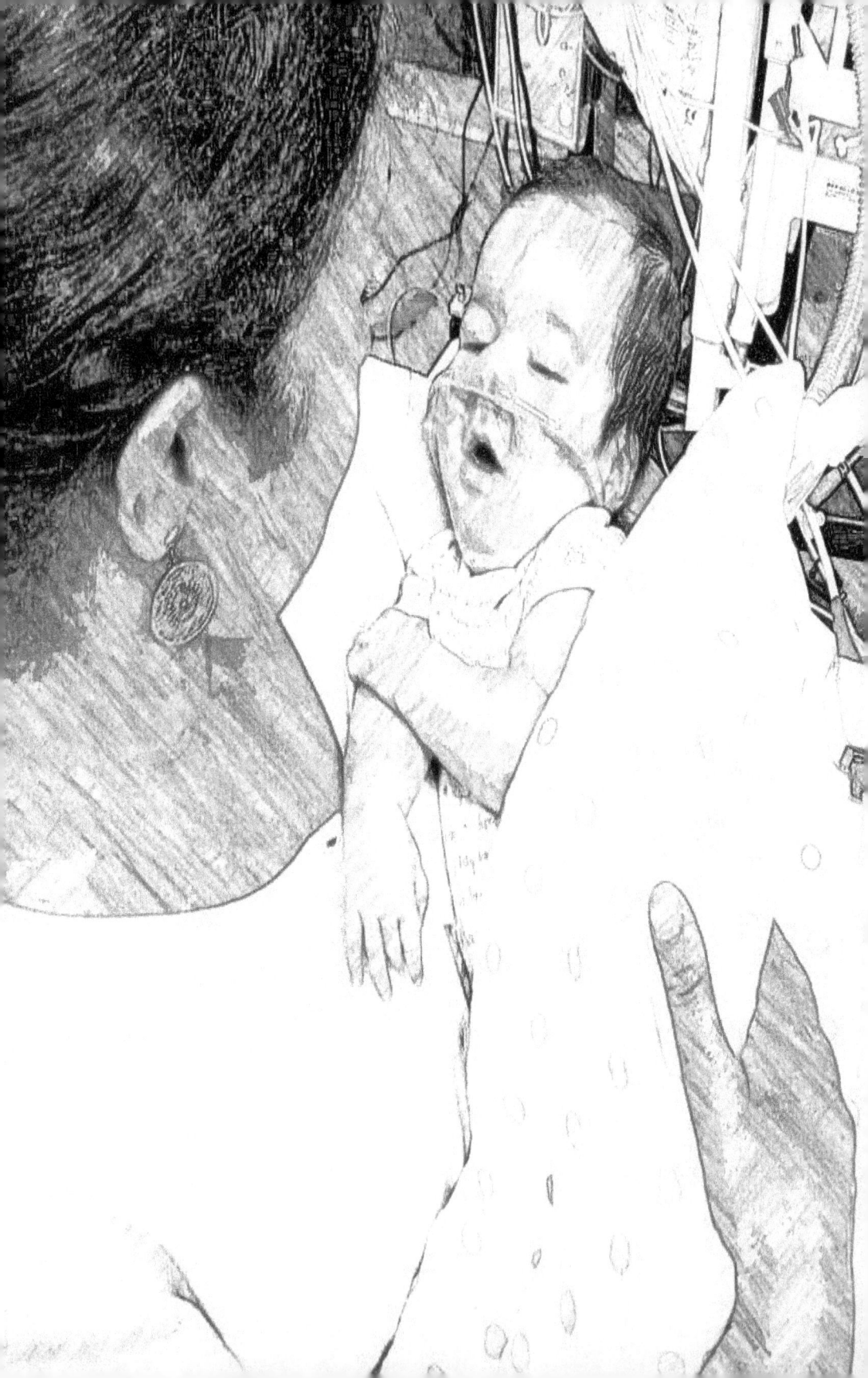

My grandma and I had a serious conversation and I paid a lot of attention. She said that she needed to go soon and that she's going to miss me and I will feel it too, but she promised me that she's going to come back. Just as well! She told me that she has to go back to work, to her house, to go back to my uncles and aunts, her friends, to my cousin B, who's also a baby. Well, not so tiny as me. She explained to me just why she's going away and I understood. In other words, it was a little difficult for me to say good-bye to her.

Since I was born, I've learned that every day is a new day and with it a new hope is born.

I have learned that my family is strong, and that's why I was born in it.

I have also learned that each baby born in this world has a mission to carry out. And that sometimes things don't come out as we planned, but we must always be grateful.

I'm finishing my diary today, saying that I very much want everyone to be well, primarily my mommy and daddy. And if it's not too much to ask, for everyone to also pray for them and send a lot of positive energy for them to keep being very strong, courageous, and determined.

A superkiss from

Luke

Ps.: Grandma! Have a good trip. I love you grandma!

Diary of a baby 11

I haven't written for a long time and I thought: *I have to update my diary.* I'm now writing here at home, and there's no place in the world better than our little corner and together with the one you love.

For me to get home an ambulance had to help transport me. Mommy stayed alongside me, as always. A big operation was set up to transport me —and for my safety— and in the end everything was fine.

Arriving home I saw my room, pretty and all decorated with Star Wars. My daddy loves the characters in the film. My dog Bolt was waiting for me. Sure, he was a little jealous, but I understood, after all, he used to reign by himself and now we're partners.

At home, finally! It's a lot more comfortable. Sure, a hospital team had to come here to organize the space so everything would be in place for me and working properly. Monitoring machines would follow me at home. That's okay!

Now I can explain a little about my illness. Keep in mind that I'm still a little baby.

Everyone knows that I had various tests until they discovered what was happening. Then came the diagnosis. A rare muscle disease called Nemaline Myopathy (hey, what a hard name to say) that meant significant problems for me.

Nemaline myopathy is a rare genetic muscle disorder that causes some peculiar things. It's a rare disease for which there's still no cure, and which is in the research stage. I think everyone knows that researching a disease is a very complex job. It may take a little time for scientists to find the cure, but they are trying and need to get more support. (My grandma Lilia always says I'm going to be a famous scientist!).

As a result of low muscle tone, which is caused by the disease, I still can't hold up my little neck. Nemaline myopathy causes trouble breathing, and trouble swallowing, and that's why I use a gastric tube and a non-invasive respirator. Have explained it right? I hope so!

I'm now going to talk about my parents. My daddy is one of these incredible guys, ever-optimistic who doesn't spare any effort for everything to come out right. I love my daddy! I think I've already said that, but it's always good to repeat. My mommy is one of these tireless women who is always investigating into some way of improving my condition. I love my mommy!

My daddy and mommy are just incredible and are doing various things with me, as always. They play, they make me smile, they're loving and caring.

Did you know that my daddy is an inventor? When he isn't working he tries to make some innovation or improve what comes readymade, so that I can be every more active. I support all his ideas. I think he wants to set up a gym for me, because sometimes he has an exercise bar in my crib, full of rings and cords. Isn't he the greatest?

Daddy and mommy also bought a float for my neck and I can be in the water flapping arms and legs. I look like a fish but when I come out of the water then comes that lousy gravity, as my mother says. Okay, okay! We'll solve this any day.

These days my mommy was playing with me, and I turned my little neck for the first time. I managed to turn it to one side and the other. Mother loved it and the more she said "Good job". I turned again and again. I did it five times. I'm acquiring lots of skills.

My mommy is still pumping her milk for me and this is my daily nourishment. What I'd really like would be to be able to nurse from her breast, but I understand that it isn't possible.

This has been a lot of writing today. Thank you for reading me. Until the next diary entry. Stay well!

With love.

Luke

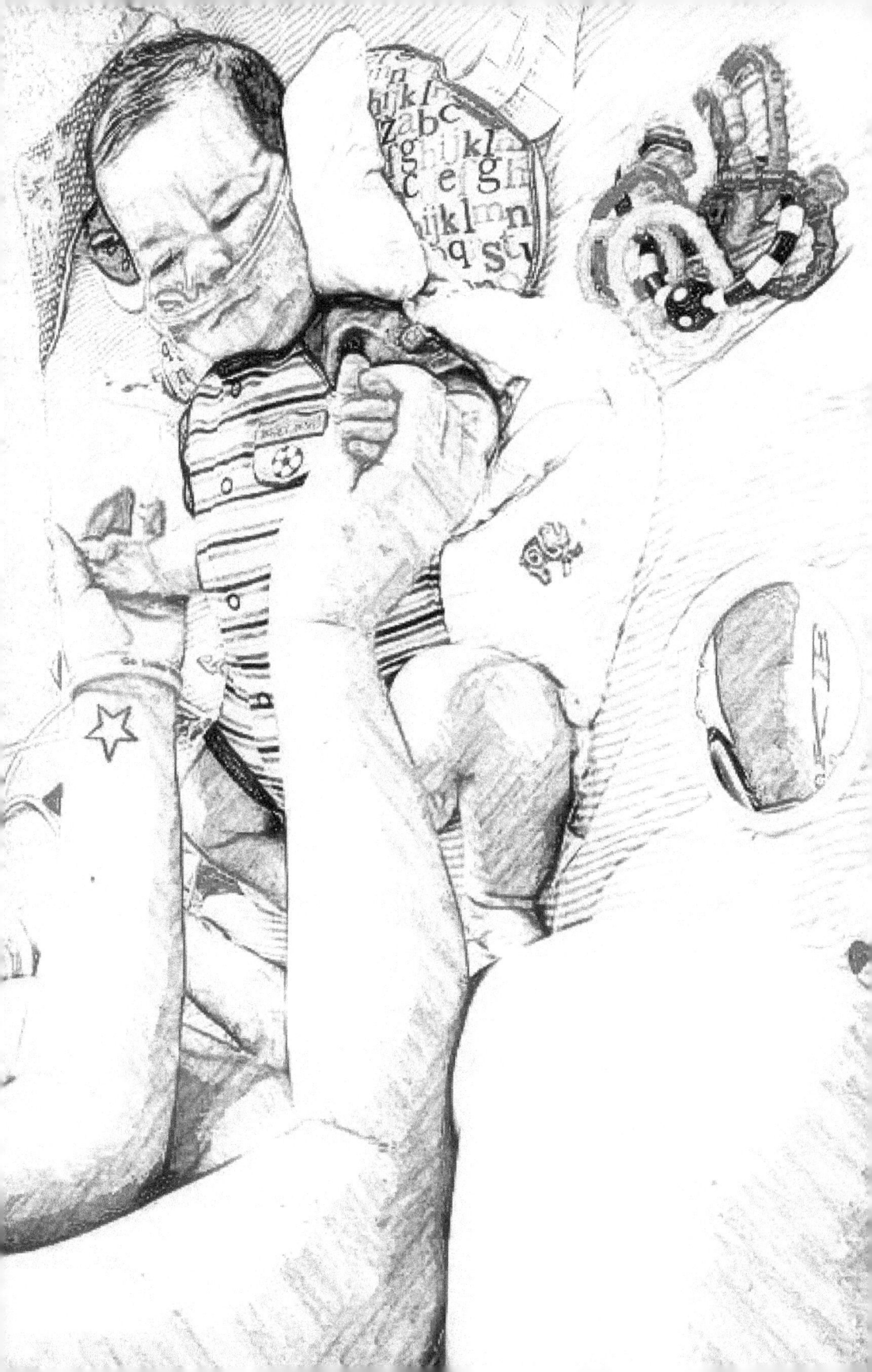

Diary of a baby 12

In December my grandmas came to visit me. Having a grandma is cool. They also play with you, sing, read, offer suggestions like: put on socks, better cover the baby (even when they feel hot), talk about being careful with the breeze outside, with mosquitoes.... a whole lot of things. They're overzealous but who doesn't like being pampered? I think grandparents are a kind of angel, except without wings.

That first Christmas I had to go back to *Joe DiMaggio Children's Hospital* in Hollywood, a city here in Florida. My grandma said that this Hollywood isn't as glamorous as the one in California, part of Los Angeles. Grandma says strange things, but that's fine. What's important is that the city has this incredible hospital and that it has fully supported me and my parents.

And as my grandma always says, the men in our family are strong and I soon went back home.

There in the hospital, the doctors thought I needed greater pressure in ventilation. So I started using a mask. It helps me sleep and expand my lungs more. Now I'm a masked man —in the good sense.

Speaking about the mask, what's nice is when my mommy takes it off. She does a delicious massage on my face, and I love it.

I know that I'm a lot of work for my parents, because they're always attentive, with their eyes on me 24 hours a day. But I think this care is what daddies and mommies do. They're my superheroes!

LILIA MONTEIRO

I sometimes realize that my mommy is sad and that makes me feel so bad, but I'm always trying to do funny little things to make her happy.

I think I understand all mommies, and my own even better. Taking care of a child isn't easy, and with my challenges it's even more work. You know, when I look at my mommy and she looks at me, I think about the huge love existing between us. What I want is to have the strength to lift my tiny arms more, to wrap her in a strong hug and to show all the love I feel for her. I have faith that one day I'll do that. Meanwhile I always open a big smile when I see her.

I keep saying that my daddy is a very cool guy and that's what he is. He prepared a garden, planted flowers and fruit trees, he wrote my name and the word "love"! The garden is on the left side of the house, and my mommy said that he did it on this side just so that I can see it from the window in my room. My daddy thinks of everything. My mommy says that he is "the best". And I believe it.

We're now in February and many things have happened since then. So, I'm going to tell about it in the next few diary entries.

Thanks again for all the positive energy, for the prayers and for the love you send me, even from afar.

A super-hug.

With love.

Luke

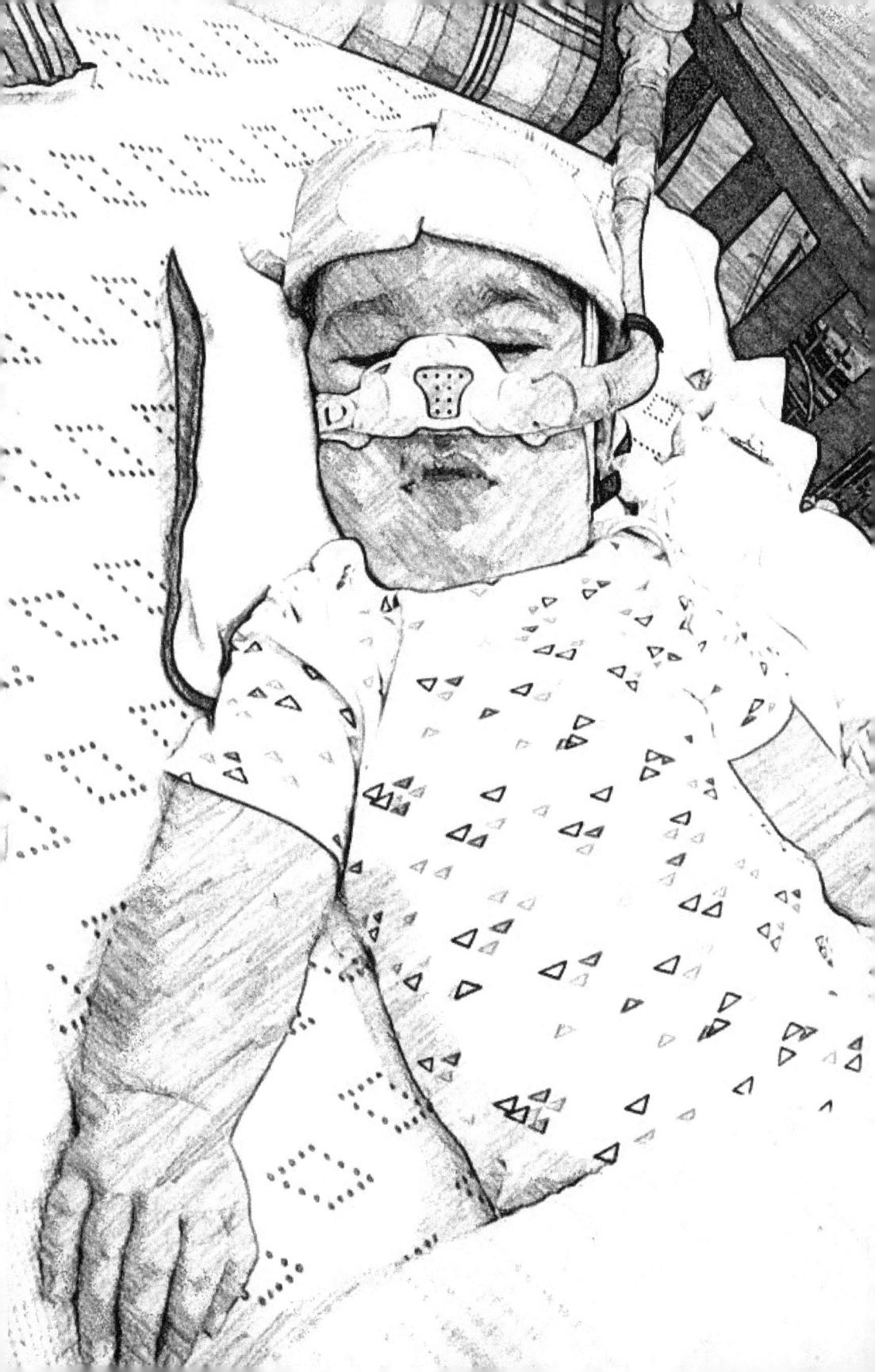

Diary of a baby 13

As you know, I'm now in the hospital, but I'd like to share a little of my routine before coming here.

I have to admit that being cared for by several specialist physicians has some advantages. I get to go out of the house often, go riding and riding in the car and meet different people. On my list of physicians is the specialist in Nemaline Myopathy; the pediatrician, whom my parents love and I do too; the gastroenterologist, the pulmonologist and the neurologist. I also go to see a respiratory therapist (I'll talk about this respiratory therapy some other time).

At home I do sessions with a physical therapist, an occupational therapist, a developmental therapist and with a speech therapist. Lots of stuff, right? Some days I end up very tired. Whew!

These days I went into an orthopedic clinic. There they produce custom orthopedic devices, and they made a kind of support so my little legs would be stretched out more. Also some booties for my feet, a vest (for strengthening my backbone), and now a support for my little hands. Lots of devices are necessary for my development, and when my parents put them all on, I end up looking like a little robot.

You know, I love to ride around in a car, but transporting me means a bit of work. My parents start the mission of getting everything ready. In the car seat my mommy places a pillow and blankets. Everything so my backbone won't hurt. They bring all those machines that beep when something is wrong. I know, I know! —they're for my safety. The little backpack with food for me has to be there. Everything ready, it's my turn to go out to the car.

I have to go lying down, because I still can't sit up. My superdad adjusts everything so I'll travel safely. He fastens the seatbelt, tightens here and there. Ready! Let's go riding!!! Okay, we're going to the doctor, but as my mommy says, it's still an outing and even a journey, because some doctors visits are in other cities.

When we get to the clinic, everything comes out again. My father or my mother put me on the stroller, hang on the machines, and we go to the visit.

Sometimes, in some visits, I get some shots on my legs and of course I cry. It's the vaccinations. My grandma often says that I'm very sensitive. I do feel it but then it goes away, after all vaccines are necessary for our protection.

The time for leaving is the best part. We go back to the car and drive. When I don't sleep, because the car's suspension makes a noise, I'm looking at everything my eyes can see, and my grandma keeps saying that I'm very smart. Grandma always has great things to say about me!

I'm always getting visits from my parents' friends, and for New Years my family came to visit me. At least part of them. It was very nice to have the house full of people. And it's also very nice to have cousins. I still don't know all of them, but those that visited me are very nice-looking and skillful. Too bad they went away. I was enjoying all that activity. I very much want to visit them some day. I think it's going to be very cool. Besides, I plan to visit and meet lots of people in Brazil.

I still have a long road to go with my parents. I know and feel that many people are rooting for us, for my health, and I'm very grateful to each one. Thanks for reading my diary and for the kind messages that you write me.

Big hug!

Luke

LILIA MONTEIRO

Diary of a baby 14

Folks!!! So much news!

Did you know I went to the hospital four times in two weeks?

Those were tough nights for my parents. The paramedics were called and they were at my house twice. Both times they came very fast and my room was full of very big people.

The second time, I was really in trouble, they took me to the hospital and even blocked traffic so I could pass by. I felt very important. Okay, for my parents, I'm very important.

I'm now at *Joe DiMaggio*, that hospital I told you about that is very very cool. They discovered what was tormenting me.

I know that my respiratory condition tires me out a lot, and my parents do everything to help me. Have you heard of something called "cough assist"? It's a respiratory therapy and it helps me to cough and clean out my lungs. There's also a little device that massages your chest and ribs. My grandma says it looks like a tiny motorcycle.

My parents now know how to identify my signs, and when things are getting tough. For breathing, right? Okay I'm almost eight months old and daddies and mommies know their children like no one else. And that's so cool!

After so much coming and going, my daddy and mommy needed to make an important decision.

Talking here, opinion there, and it was still hard to decide. Parents always think of what is best for us, right? But let's agree, drilling a hole in a baby's neck can't be an easy decision.

Finally, they decided that I really needed a tracheostomy.

Lots of prayer, lots of positive energy, I know, came from so many people, and from various places on the day of the surgery, and it worked.

And here I am, with a necklace, no mask and a more comfortable condition. Admiring my pretty mommy, who doesn't move from my side. Smiling at my daddy more than ever. Paying lots of attention to my grandma and to her camera and to all the people who are at my side doing what has to be done.

I still have some weeks in the hospital to recover well and so that my parents can be trained to deal with the tra-che-os-to-my (hard word...) but I know soon they will also have this under their belt, they my superheroes, and then, folks, I go back home.

Thanks, thanks, thanks!

I love all of you!

Affectionately, here's my hooray!

Luke

Diary of a baby 15

My 45 days in the hospital were busy, and finally I came back home thirteen days ago.

As I told you, my parents needed to be well trained to deal with my tracheostomy, since the procedure is rather complicated and it has to be done with a lot of care.

I'm still doing respiratory therapy, but now only with a tiny light hammer, which helps clean my lungs. It doesn't hurt at all, but my grandma always feels affected by it, thinking that I may be suffering some pain. At home, no motorcycle, just the little hammer.

My parents' first training session was done with a doll, similar to a little baby, and it had a hole in its neck just like mine.

To deal with my tracheostomy you have to use light white gloves on both hands, and nothing, absolutely nothing, can touch those gloves except the tube which is going to be placed in my trachea to remove the secretion. It's a good idea that there always be two persons to do this. But my daddy and my mommy can now do it by themselves. Since I collect a lot of secretion, cleaning is done several times a day. Now I don't have any doubt that my parents are really my superheroes.

The hardest procedure is changing the necklace, which is done once a day. That's when there always have to be two people. And my parents are getting more and more efficient at this.

LILIA MONTEIRO

Do you know that my daddy did a tracheostomy on my Chewbacca and then on Master Yoda? I don't know how he managed to perform the two surgeries, I only know that I was right there and I saw everything. My daddy said that my friends wanted to show solidarity with me, and everything was fine with them.

With the tracheostomy I can see all around me and I observe my parents' every step. We are all adapting to this new situation, and despite all the problems that my nemaline myopathy imposes on me, I know that I'm a baby very much loved by my parents, by my grandmas and grandpas, my uncles and aunts, and a whole lot of people that I still haven't met.

I am happy and thankful for the parents I chose and that God has given me. When I see them smiling, saying that they love me so much, taking care of me with so much affection —mommy always researching something to make me conformable, and my daddy, tireless, always inventing things to help me get stronger— I can only show thanks with my smile, because I know that they love it.

That's all for today and I still need to take advantage of the last days with my grandma, because she is going to go away again, but I know she'll come back.

Superkiss.

With love,

Luke

Diary of a baby 16

When I look at my parents and observe them carefully, I can feel the intensity of this magnificent and special love that they feel for me and how much they understand me.

There are times, when I'm feeling some pain or discomfort —when I express myself however I can or am able. But my parents know. My heart rate speeds up, the adrenalin rises, the sweat comes, and the tears as well.

I know they will do everything to improve this temporary discomfort. My parents read me. I know!

I'm not able to do some things but perhaps I think about them, how to strive —and how I try!

I like music, I like when my grandma dances in front of me and talks with me! She watches me intently and wants me to win! It's double love this grandma love. I like clapping, smiles, sweet and tender words. Yes, I like that! And my family provides me all that. And even knowing my limitations, we remain determined.

I ask myself whether when I grow up I will be stronger.

Many things go on in my mind. My brain works but my muscles ... —they're still not able to go along with it as it should be.

I try with all my might to begin some sound. Do you hear me! I ask my parents. Yes, they hear me. They know that I'm trying to speak to them somehow.

When my mother looks at me and kisses me in a way that only mothers do, I'm dazzled and I think: *how I'd like to hug you and kiss you the way you do it.*

I see my mother going away and lose sight of her. I see her coming back and with all her charm, she makes me break out in a smile. My best smile!

My father comes and he sings, he makes me happy, he communicates security —the certainty that I'm always going to be able to count on him soothes me.

My love for my parents only increases. And that is magic!

So, I'm convinced that my strength comes from God —someone far superior to all things. My strength comes from my family which takes care of me like a rare crystal and communicates this unconditional love to me.

With love,

Luke

www.ingramcontent.com/pod-product-compliance
Lightning Source LLC
Chambersburg PA
CBHW031530040426
42445CB00009B/467